# TOTEM: AMERICA

# TOTEM: AMERICA

*poems by*

Debra Kang Dean

TIGER BARK PRESS ❀ ROCHESTER, NEW YORK ❀ 2018

Published by Tiger Bark Press,
202 Mildorf Ave., Rochester, NY 14609.

Design by Philip Memmer.

Cover art (top image):
INDIE FOLKFEST
EPHEMERAL COMMUNITY ART PROJECT
2018. Acrylic on wood, 72 × 96 inches.
Mennello Museum of American Art, Orlando, Florida.
Photo by Robin Lippincott.

ISBN-13: 978-0-9976305-9-6

Publication of this book made possible with public funds from the New York State Council on the Arts with the support of Governor Andrew M. Cuomo and the New York State Legislature.

*for my son David*

# Table of Contents

# VOTIVE

Like Horatio,
as fate or chance or
luck would have it—

vigilance, the watch
word I say, O say
do you mind while I

stand here, mind the gap
between desire and
fulfillment. Meanwhile,

do not mistake it.
Mark you. We are here:
This is a story.

A love story.

# THE APPLE

At the health food store
past clear bins of beans,

grains, among the kitchenware,
she found displayed

a dappled Gala,
a cross-pollinated

offspring of Red and
Golden Delicious.

Only a tomato,
except for the leafy

tuft at its stem end, seemed
at a glance as real.

Leafless, untouched,
the apple looked so real.

Past temptation's first
bite, it was scary.

The waxy fruit fooled
even the painter,

my friend, who handed
over the apple.

Said, "You bit."

# JAM

crushed, the press of
bodies: sugar
sweetened fruit or
bored teens, flesh smushed
into a phone
booth's fused seams: his
hurt finger, the
berry-like bruise
on her thin wrist:
this little im-
provisation
this little twist:
a heedless, turn-
about to face
head on a gust
that wheezes back
in the raspy
voice of grinding
gears, of the ob-
scene phone caller,
of frayed cables,
of your breathless
exhalations:
hold it, hold the
elevator
could you please hold

# IRASHAIMASSE

A vacant metal box we
Fill with our bodies.
In white gloves and pillbox hat
She walks forward to press us back.

She steps back, bows as the doors
Slide to close before us.
Muzak, sluggish and boring
As we are, still adores us:

"Close to You," all sweet violins.
Hard not to think about the perfect
Karen Carpenter and her perfect wooden
Drumming in the biopic.

This is the sorry ascent
To the rooftop garden: pulleys and cables
Displacing air, fluorescent
Bulbs blinking in the starless crucible.

Or perhaps it is really all descent,
Where we'll finger the latest sales,
To lose ourselves in the bargain basement's
Clamor of red-tagged designer labels.

*Write it down*, the Old Bat implores,
But my fountain pen's clogged.
I touch the nib to my tongue.
It leaves a black mark there.

# SINGLE-LENS REFLEX

These twitches, the mind's reflex—
as if out of the soil, memory's crop
pushing its way up, each persistent shoot
lifting aside what burden to unreel
itself to light? I have seen a bulb blow up
or so it seemed, filmed in time lapse. Exposed,

here, I'm recalling an exposé
on the tube. Run's the body's reflex.
In my mind's eye, a close up turns blow up
of a thin man with close-cropped
dark hair mouthing a scream—so unreal
my mouth's mouthing, *Don't shoot.*

Who do I think I am. A bystander, I shoot
rolls of film, prints over-exposed
like the theater's black-and-white newsreels
my child self counted backwards with, a reflex.
The mind's a land mine, a bird's crop
stopped up, sometimes threatening to blow up.

How many months before the final blow up
had I made up my mind to shoot
from the hip? He wouldn't nip or crop
each grievance this time. My ex posed.
I hugged my pillow, knees tucked, a reflex
to try to stay the room's mad reeling.

Today, the world seems a little surreal.
A girl in a pink dress blows up
a green balloon—or tries to. Its reflex
is to contract. Sucking used air, "Shoot,"
she chokes. She grins, exposes
black space, baby teeth a harvested crop.

My camera flashes. Time will crop
the photographs, do what I will. I reel
the film back till the first exposure's
swallowed up. Already memory's blow up
of this moment is being developed. "Oh, shoot,"
I sigh, but too late to short circuit the reflex.

Sometimes I fear smoke is my true crop. It blows up-
ward and dissipates. I can't reel it in, can't shoot
to a stand down this bent, this exposed-by-now reflex.

# BURNING. LOVE.

## I.

When Elvis offered himself to the waiting world,
*a hunk of burning love*, we couldn't foresee
his burn out in the end. Back then
when he crooned *love me tender*,
girls swooned as if the words lighting his lips
were kisses. My older sister, then sixteen, wild
with bright red lipstick, warned me a woman
like Doris Day was destined to fade out
or die a virgin. My sister longed to be
a struck match, burning, to hurt so hot
she'd have to wrench each love letter from her heart
like a suicide note. And me? In secret
I stood in front of a full-length mirror
awkwardly shaking my straight and narrow hips.
Barely eleven, I'd yet to know the stirrings
in that vacancy of flesh, my soft center
where in two years' time, the first letting
of blood would initiate my own brand of burning.

## II.

Three years ago, on the anniversary of Elvis's death,
I lifted the ritual glass of cranberry juice on the rocks
that my friend would only serve me with vodka.
"To the King of Rock 'n' Roll," I said.
"No, No," she said, and offered instead a toast
to the urinary-tract infection. It gave us need
for such tasty medicinals as this Cranberry Mist.
I confess, it was the spirits we were after. Two drinks
and then my friend's slow unreeling: "I hated
those bastards drove my father North
till I touched the grooves worn into my oldest
sister's skin, load after load of cotton she shouldered
hunching her still-child's body down.
What does it matter? My father and sister
are both dead. A toast to those hooded bastards
who torched a sharecropper's fields in Tennessee
and left my body to stand upright."
She puffed on then put down her cigarette.
"Girl, Elvis had nothing on me," she said,
already standing, and, "Watch my hips."
We laughed until our eyes stung from the smoke
of her father's fields, burning.

## III.

Three months ago my woodstove backpuffed
and singed the hair around my face. When touched,
like dead leaves, my burnt hair, curled and brittle,
broke just shy of where the heat died out.
For several days my eyelids stung like sunburn.
For several weeks I sometimes woke to the smell
of my own hair burning. I know this
is nothing. I know a six-year-old's whole being
was partly consumed by fire. His father
meant for them to die like lovers. Love makes
the father tell his son as he strikes
the match, "If I can't have you, no one can."
This part, I tell you, is true. Too late
the child's crazed dancing and the smell of burning
flesh will call the father back to his senses.
We have seen this before. Only here our lovers
are father and son: In a hotel room,
the father, himself burning with love,
holding the lit match that will give
his beautiful son a mask of grafted skin
for a face. The child, burning.

# THE TONGUE DEPRESSOR

"Ask your mother," the shrink says,
But I don't want to know
About the dream of lost keys,
Not today; it is too, too cold.

And I don't want to know
The corpse count, the wind chill.
Not today, it is too cold.
I am the dropbox filled.

The corpse count, the wind chill
Cools even the hide bound.
I am the dropbox filled
With not one single video rewound.

Cooled, even the hide bound,
Tongue-tied, bleary-eyed dictator—
And not one single video yet rewound.
I call him Old Spud, Mr. Tater.

The tongue-tied, bleary-eyed dictator
Says, "Ah," for the tongue depressor.
I call him Old Spud, Mr. Tater,
Spit and curse. Then bite my tongue,

And say, "Ah," for the tongue depressor.
"In the dream of lost keys
No spite cures. Bite your tongue."
That's what my mother says.

# ODE TO THE BROWN-HEADED COWBIRD

Brood parasite of those passerines,
with your leather-like hood,
your iridescent black body,

neither the plagiarist of the aviary nor
the sequined harlequins are as reviled
by lovers of songbirds as you are.

The notes of your song fall first like water's
then like a jackhammer's. You sing
and listen, wait for that come-hither

wing stroke, subtle as a Noh
gesture, draw closer, sing
a different melody, then again

draw closer. How many songs
have you sung, must you
sing for that brief cloacal kiss?

In this, your first season after
the plagues of failure, you will
finally taste success.

Forty eggs will your mate lay
each in a different nest—warbler's,
red-winged blackbird's, junco's . . .

If not turned out or pecked open,
they will hatch offspring
already skilled in begging. And now,

reformed delinquent, from this day forward
free as a bird you will stay.
After a year perfecting technique

and learning to look and listen,
you have arrived, winged Philoctetes.
Who wouldn't envy you?

# LITTLE FLY

One crow staggers like a drunk in Jamaica Plain,
One crow staggers on the road and collapses—
It is our canary: West Nile or Eastern equine,
    La Crosse or St. Louis encephalitis.

You touch the wheal on your clammy arm,
You touch the sign where she has pierced you—
For heat and light, for breath and perspiration
    She kept searching till she found you.

If the sensory nerve to her abdomen
Were cut, if it were, she'd still keep sucking
Up through her proboscis, needle thin,
    Until she burst. Too much isn't enough.

Cover up. Don't let water stagnate. Or
Stay inside. Cover up against the coming fray:
Malaria, dengue and yellow fever,
    Headache, muscle ache, general malaise.

# THE BOG

Below the dull sheen of Ms. Pogany's
dark hair tightly drawn back, a face
all eyes, eerily alien
                 seen dead on

—because light distorts and
clarifies: as when a woman,

embarked on an easy hike,
breaks her ankle,
                 the unforgiving
shoe having wedged itself in the roots

of a tree. Something between a wince
and a howl escapes her lips

as the EMTs ease her
                      onto the stretcher.
One had lashed himself to a tree
on the steep slope to help lift her

away from the water.
One cuts the laces of her shoe

to free her foot,
                 its weight
dog legging the line from her shin
before he fastens the brace.

Over and over again she asks after
the shoe: "You don't need to

cut it, do you?
                        You aren't going to
cut it off, are you? You
didn't cut it, did you?" until,

mending done, one shows her
the shoe. The other turns

away from the bog.
                        She cradles the shoe
                        as they raise her up.

# CONFESSIONAL

If you're holding the charts
that map out the constellations
while looking to name a few stars,
say, Altair, Vega, Aldebaran, or

if you're searching
for cartoonish explosions,
for remix or parody on the screen,
maybe this isn't for you.

I'm serious. (I've been told
I'm too serious.) Sorry. In truth,
I don't mean *I'm sorry*;
I just want an unlocked gate

to swing on the hinge of those words.
When I say I put down my cat last month,
I'm not talking about talking.
I mean I shut the gate. I mean

at four in the morning I woke to the sound
of distress—slow after nineteen years,
I did finally learn to hear it—
and held him through a seizure,

a fissure the self he was slipped through.
After which, for him, all of life was refusal.
I called the vet. I put him in the carrier
I called the Death Car after I put down

my other cat—to own my actions.
Don't ask me to name my cats.
If you're still with me, perhaps
you're thinking, *Christ, they're just cats.*

Well, after the fact, thought/said
some of the onlookers and virtual
onlookers watching two women
putting each other down, *Catfight.*

"Bitch," one woman had said. "Fuck you.
You're stupid," the other repeated. And then
the first punch. Then clawing and
a prying loose. *Christ, it's just a seat.*

It's a seat on the bus where
the people go 'round and 'round.
If you were listening, I think
you know what I mean. Perhaps

it's why we're unapologetic. I know
I'm being a hypocrite: This is
a virtual sound of grief turned
grievance—and that is my grief.

The last gasps rattle a body.
I know. Remember my cat?
Rumor has it departing souls
like the hottest stars burn blue.

In the language of fists,
it's red, a cheek flames red.
It's a sorry sight. Sorry,
I'm saying, Sorry.

# AN OPEN EYE

There's no explaining what
it means, in a single instant
finding and losing a friend,

not once but twice.
I know that Death, like God,
wears many faces,

but the heart, indiscriminate,
only hammers out its
one note. When I close

my fingers, I need not
imagine the size of the heart
delivering the blows that wake me.

A cubit, that measure
from elbow to fingertip—how
imprecisely human it is,

but close enough, I'd say,
to measure the two-by-two
scale of Noah's ark.

Really, it isn't the shock
that I survived, but the after-
shocks reminding me

I survived. Shock,
like God, is merciful, and,
like God, it is wrathful too.

Nearly twenty-five years after
his friend nicked off
a piece of my son's finger

with a rock—boys
pounding rocks with rocks—
I can still see the notch,

the flesh of his finger cleanly
removed like a slice of pie—
my mind kept trying

to put it back
as blood spilled first
down to the floor then

into a dishcloth,
my mouth saying calmly,
"Tight, hold your finger

tight, Sweetie," even as,
for his sake, my wavering voice
did not break. I'm beginning

to understand the temptation
to call a patient in a vegetative state
a potted plant. How

through sickness and death,
could you go on
if you didn't?

I'm thinking of calling myself
the Black Widow. I'm thinking
I'll get a really deep tan.

I'm thinking of weaving a net
of words big as a fumigation tent,
of embroidering two

large Ds that I'll wear
like a sandwich board
whenever I go out. I'm thinking

I'll haunt the malls,
a modern-day Hester
embellishing her punishment

so it openly declares a distant
but stately lover's name—
though really, at heart, I know

I am living under the sign
of an open eye, this cipher
"I" a stand-in for the name

that becomes me:
Ishmael, call me
Ishmael.

# MEDICINE BALL

I think that's what it's called,
that half-deflated leather ball
a man keeps ahead of him with a blow
delivered dead on with toe-tip.
A dull thud, like a body struck,
and it dribbles a few feet. It's not luck
that steers its course, but the man's
intent, sure as a train track.
It's in the odd angle of his left arm,
the hand stiffly suspended, that you know
some harm has befallen him—stroke?
heart attack?—you know he is
a thing refusing brokenness.
You read it in the set of his jaw,
the barrel chest that squares his shoulders
as he shuffles just inside the paved path.
You, too, have come to the park
in the aftermath of your own disaster.
Thump, and the ball inches to a rest
just beyond the bench where you imagine
yourself for the first time taking
a long drag on a cigarette. Sublime.
It's the only word that describes
the billowy clouds, their tops backlit
against a sky the same blue as
your man's eyes, already deepening
into a melancholier blue. Thump.
The man passes before you.
He does not look up. Periwinkle?
Cornflower? Orchid, perhaps?

You don't have a name for it yet.
So you write this down
while there's still a little light.

# HIT

Just a hint of smoke
inside the frame the lens makes—

ignoring this small detail,
intent on one figure,

I might have thought
he was just clowning now—

though why so close to
the finish line, I couldn't tell—

this athlete wracked by spasms,
arms folding and flapping

like the wings of
a raptor I saw, talons sunk

into a catch that the water
sucked back down.

Not until the third time
playing it back, do I see

the concussive blows,
the man hit and hit

by a force as yet unseen,
against which his body

tries to right itself,
with each one, his knees

being knocked out
from under him,

the collapse backwards,
in his fall denied even

a suggestion of prayer.
Think of it: he's one

of the lucky ones,
looking as if he's escaped

with his body intact—
though maybe already

taking shape the stigmata
of scrapes or bruises where

flesh and asphalt met.
If he doesn't

speak, it isn't
because he's mute.

Outside the window,
against a sky freighted

with clouds, a flag waves.
At half-mast a flag waves.

# "OF THEE I SING"

*[B]efore release of composite sketches of two John Does, there
was a widespread assumption, fueled by media speculation,
that the horrific act in America's heartland had to be the work
of Middle Eastern terrorists. People on the street talked about
their renewed suspicion of foreigners. One called the bombing
a declaration of war, not unlike Pearl Harbor.*
            —David Maraniss, *The Washington Post*


*"Don't be upset, José Alberto, . . . I'm only crying in English."*
            —Elizabeth Bishop in Brazil

Not long after news of the Oklahoma City bombing broke,
I thought, *It's déjà vu all over again!* the grief in my throat
like acid reflux, what could I do
                     but laugh. I thought
of a friend's mother in Michigan, part of a group
of Iranian-Americans *large enough to constitute a minority.*

When he and I first met near Ōsaka, Americans hadn't yet topped
critical mass; people were curious. He was free
to be thoroughly American,
                    getting a waitress's attention
by playing a cowboy accent for all it was worth: "Sue-me-
maah-sin," he'd say, or "Auh-re-gaah-toe"—then break

into real Japanese, fluently casual, unlocking
the waitress's eyes from mine, turning her mouth
(half-frown, half-grimace)
                into a smile. There,
he didn't mind being a foreigner. I, on the other hand,
till a sip of beer or my native tongue betrayed me,

could and liked being invisible. But I confess
I sometimes sought out "modern" restaurants just to listen
to American music.
                    I once watched him close the distance
between himself and a group of schoolboys working  up
the nerve then chanting, "Gaijin, Gaijin"; and he starting to hop

and sway from side to side, keeping their rhythm,
his arms tense and shivering in mock delight,
then advancing, pointing,
                              chanting back,
"Nihon-jin, Nihon-jin," running, the boys
craning their necks backwards and squealing.

Having been talked into taping and watching reruns
of "Cheers" and packing more than once from the States—
nearly half way 'round the world,
                              in fact!—bagfuls
of Combos, boxes of Pop Tarts, I know why
he makes a model of Sam Malone. Incorrigible

womanizer, he translates that challenge into charming
free meals from strangers—and friends, too.
I knew his game
                    and liked him in spite of it.
Sometimes what comes back is the sound
of his feet shuffling against the tiled walk

as we made our way through a mall near Takatsuki
Hankyu-station. I pause to look back, see his wrists,
limp above his pointy
                              elbows, and, on a day
neither of us knows what to make of our lives,
he's leaning against me, saying, "Carry me."

But it's recalling the incongruity and utter compatibility
of the last meal we shared before I stopped
my transpacific visits
                              that turned the weather forecast
into background noise: before us on the table,
a dozen dishes portioned in servings no bigger than

a mouthful, weird compromises of Eastern and Western
cuisine whose names escape me—I know it's wrong
but I want to say "enoki pizza" or
                              "Texas-style sushi"
to give you the flavor of it. To my grazer's delight,
we ate and ate, keeping each other in beer

in a country where only the intemperate pour their own,
where this simple act could mean, "Here, your glass
is nearly empty" or "Please,
                              my glass is nearly empty"—
and talked until he turned, as I knew he would,
to the question he would ask me each time I met him:

"After so many years, aren't you tired of living
with the same person?" Outside the glass wall
of the restored

                    eighteenth-century structure,
its thatched roof weathered but intact, was a garden
so carefully constructed, it seemed perfectly natural.

And a tiny waterfall. And under the waterfall,
a bamboo dipper—the kind you might see at temples—
that filled then see-sawed empty,

                    *Clunk . . . clink,*
then started to fill again. Pointing, I said, "It's like that."

# FILIGREE

i.

unfolded like paper

the sky : dispersed grains

particles of seeded clouds

how falling rain scars

& glosses what remains

glazes each loss : a golden

clot : a dry well papered

the cerebral cortex ingrained

a wind maze of cloud-

traces & the same starry scar-

flecked veil the remaindered

tender of sluiced gold

or fool's gold this paper-

thin grief this grosgrain

ribbon strung up to cloud

the dome above Madagascar

where no snow falls : slim remains

famished amid the slicked : & gilded

ii.

One among the slickly gilded—
delivered of memory's cloud

a missive: the leprous pauper
near a Hong Kong plaza, a scar,

a knot against the smooth grain
of foot traffic. He remains

in eyeshot, unbanished, where gold
chains hang on mannequins clad

in spun silks, confetti peppering
their stiff feet. Sunlight scores

their angled poses, darkens groins
cocked hips suggest. They're meant

to express a cheerful mind geld,
fake hair, fake flesh, a fair clod

thinly dimensioned, blank paper
no lead has touched, eraser scoured.

Or so I thought until one twitched. Grounded,
the leper, sole bent skyward, remanded us.

iii.


Soul bent skyward, Milton reminds us
of figurative, buried talents light scarcely
touches through veil of mind fog or cloud,
through the heart, God seared.

After the scabbing over a scar
appears. It's time to pull the clown-
suit over the self's tattered remains.
Who needs clout?

& yet doubt lingers. The newspaper
is full of true accounts, field goals
that elicit oohs but also fray the grain
because news goads

one to the task: there's still sweet gold
hereabouts for the drone. Paper's
for maps to lost treasure grown
mythical once enpapered.

"Life's tautological," B. said. "Remain
patient. Practice your engrams."

iv.


Patience to practice,
    to form an engram, perseverance, persistence to engrain
in muscle memory complex patterns,
    three square, four chambered, a kind of cud-
chewing, a sluicing
    through finer and finer sieves for slivers of gold,
an almost airy nothing,
    a drumming drumming through each named
exertion down to toe touches—
    straight knees, ladies!—your ample torso pear-
shaped in the bodysuit
    pressing as the world presses against skin's fragile sac


out of which you wake
    to the hiss & groan of a bus disgorging its cargo in the rain,
sealed windows of vibrating cars,
    the vibrant yellow one no lemon but a loud
announcement: *I luv my skul,*
    as the high-school huffer graffitied it. Oh, I grow old,
I grow old
    on streets where deafsters come & go, even in Podunk, Maine,
for every nook in America's
    touched by the fiber-optic fabric of our lives turning paper
obsolete—though we still read
    the want ads: used furniture, fun DWMs, pre-owned cars.

"I am so tired," N. said.

In the dreamscape a gigantic face, eyes slits & lips stretched grin-thin, is a ghoulish imitation

Cheshire cat, one of the thousand nebulous cloud-screens in the jumbotronland's

gimme, showmethemoney, honey, God—

what all were we saying?

In Iraq & Afghanistan, North Korea & Iran, encased, we remain in the two-chambered vault

of men's skulls against which a mother's voice grieves: *Reap what you've sown.*

On each continent, the poisoned rivers shine like fresh scars.

v.

Navigable channels glisten like dying stars
under these neon lights in the vaporous
humors of dull tongues, the sullied refrain
of the stand-up on the platform, train
blinking its blank eye now red, now gold

through layers of haze suspended like flimsy clouds.

Strewn wrist to elbow the scatter of barbed scars
one mendicant veteran peruses like a newspaper.
Yesterday's news. Mercury vapor lights spill rain—
unstrung beads, pearl barley, Bill Bailey, grains
of light that for now, come home, to ward off the cold.

That fill the vertical spaces dividing the crowd.

*Fili-greed.* That was self-justification one crass
acquaintance uttered. Its noun, translucent as paper,
rebounded in the air, where undivided it remained
apart from action, to be carried over again
& rinsed in clear rain falling. Truth be told

it was beauty's true stand-in: *filigree*, our sad clown.

vi.

Our sad clown with his cloud
of red hair a crown remains
            our seer our sore our scar

where all glitter is fool's gold
here where pixelated grains
            evanesce without the ground of paper

Oh Bozo oh Bonzo oh Ronnie-o cloud
maker your commemorated remains
            made us nostalgic—glazed over our scared

selves with sweet sentiment's golden
light until we recalled the grainy
            black & whites of pasted-in newspaper

clippings—like grass like cataract-clouded
pupils like us grasping remaindered
            dreams after the war divided & scarred us

& still the walls are down—to gild
our privacies we re-inscribe space on paper

# READINGS

Today's hard sweeping of leaves plastered on asphalt—
  it's your fault, yesterday's taiji practice without
first sweeping dry leaves; your fault, out of the woods
  early last evening, I rode into the city—
my hours, these days, like

  those tiles framed in a square,
    where the one empty space
  allows the circuitous maneuvering
    one must do to make a picture. So
  I'm here to tell you about my Chinese

Chinese philosophy professor whose name
  escapes me though his face is clear:
horned-rim glasses, a little beak of a nose.
  Two weeks into the class, he dragged us through
some secondary text on Confucius

word by tedious word. Our eyes glazed.
  But he kept on the whole hour stuck on one
small paragraph, pausing at every noun
  and verb as if each were a diamond
he couldn't help but turn in the light.

Stopping at one point, unable to contain
  his excitement, he shouted, *I want to drive you
home*. Well, he got my attention then
  and forever—the moon, not the finger, pointing.
It's amazing how many ways one will maneuver

a tool to keep from stooping—indoors the vacuum
    passing thirty ways from Sunday over a single square
of carpet to hook a stubborn piece of thread.
    It's not rational—which calls to mind,
since I'm on the subject,

another story about him: his-three-year-old,
    asked to give back my four-year-old's toy car, throwing
a tantrum that needed no translation, my teacher shaking
    his head, smiling, and saying, *Excuse him,*
*he's not rational.* Neither was I, I guess,

with the stuck leaves and my push broom,
    each stroke further flattening the leaves
except approached from the leafstalk.
    Of course, I did stoop, finally, to pick one up.
What had been simply brown leaves

began to distinguish themselves: shagbark hickory,
    three kinds of oak, American basswood,
Norway maple, and even Asiatic bittersweet.
    These leaves, not the damp sweetness
of red and orange and still yellowing leaves

you'd stroked, loving their fullness,
    knowing them pore to breathing pore,
but rain soaked and brown. It's your fault, too,
    this stopping to note the day's variegated
shapes and veiny textures, this

momentary stay. Hello, goodbye,
    both of us already leaving the Bay State,
how else explain this *me ke aloha*?
    Come to the city for remembrances,
I heard once more a companionable voice

in exile, moved and moving, wanting
    "to drive you home." *Ave,*—no,
*salve atque vale*, is that how you say it?
    Think of me squaring the circle outdoors,
practicing, wordless, an art that touches beauty.

# BLUE SKY WITH KOI

As if to be in the heartland was not to be
        in the center but farthest removed
    from every other point—I saw this first in Art
            Sinsabaugh's photographs: homesteads
        like islands, your green sea not yet risen to flood tide.

        Not my constant sea swayed by the moon
            but a sea of expectant ears, I imagined;
    in the air the odor, the ordure, of pigs,
        and year after year that sea receding,
leaving the brittle spikes of corn stubble—

as if a rain of arrows launched toward
        heaven had broken against hard dirt. Only
    twenty years ago, I'm told, this I might have seen
            with my own eyes, just north of town
        where the college, an island continent,

        now sprawls. On this blue day, without
            a single cloud to parcel out the sky, I am
    remembering your huge hands held out
        under the waterfall that I might see
your not-yet-toddler baby girl turning her bright face,

eyes closed, away from you and toward
        the cool mist. There, inside the geodesic
    dome that is the Climatron, the familiar
            thick air pressed against each exposed pore;
        in the pungent air the faintly mildewy scent of

the home I am always but never quite leaving.
        Outside, paths in the Japanese garden, laid out
to conceal and reveal each new vista, bent and
        turned, keeping bad spirits a few steps behind us.
As if for a moment I had bathed my senses

in the floating world that memory keeps suspended
        just above this one. The day was cool and clear
and blue like this one, the slightly opaque water
        in the manmade pond still, so still, it gave us
back to ourselves as, silent, we stood on the bridge.

        But, of course, we knew such illusions can't last.
        Over the placid water you cast a handful of pellets
as if they were coins. The water roiled for an instant
        before a hundred carp troubled the water,
fins and tails propelling them forward and upward

to break the surface, each shouldering each, lipless mouths,
        like brittle parchment, fully extended, though whether
to utter a silent O or Oh, I couldn't tell. "That's chaos,"
        you said, clapping the residue of food from your hands
as the water began the slow work of righting itself,

        as we sauntered back across the bridge, and, parting,
turned away and onward toward our separate lives.

# SWEEP

She bears down on the angled broom, leans as she stoops to inspect
    The cast-off shell of a locust, the slit down the back a split so clean
You might'd think a razor had cut it. More likely, a silent explosion—
    A bag of chips squeezed into opening—
        That bore its former inhabitant into a new life
Begun with damp, crumpled wings soon fanned dry.

The plastic bristles of the broom splay like her ten toes
    Bearing her weight as she squats. How prickly the locust's
Tiny feet against her open palm. She would
        But doesn't press her tongue against it,
    Doesn't test its crispness with her teeth. Not today.
No salt there, she thinks, considering its dull translucence.

She rises instead and sets it on the sill. She begins to sweep up
    The yard's cast offs. Leaves, twigs, berries,
        The lantern-like leavings of a tree
She cannot yet name. The wind brushes the leaves,
    And soon her sweeping gathers into itself
The sound of the surf's tongues on a day like this one:

High, high up, clouds diffuse as stirred-up dust.
    Just last week, trapped in her car, rain falling so hard
        Even manic wiper blades couldn't undo
The blurry view of the world beyond the windshield.
    She'd pulled over until the storm inside her blew over.
And then she started the car again and drove the slow way home.

Or, rather, to a temporary shelter where, beyond the fence,
        The neighbor's cat scratches itself,
    Its triangular head tilted toward the hind paw darting
        Inside its ear. And then the rasp
Of its pink tongue she cannot hear. By now,
        She has given herself over to sweeping as if

This ongoing drag might counter the motion
        Of Time's relentless sweeping,
    As if in this momentary stitching
        The rent world might be held together,
As if all that had fallen away from her might be given back.

# MAY DAY

Hard to say what it is—tree,
shrub, maybe a clone, so given is it
to being grafted—yet this much
I know:
           native to every state
save one, its names are many:
sugarplum, shadbush, juneberry, even
saskatoon though the name I know

is serviceberry (in Appalachia
*service* becoming *sarvis*) because,
some fancied, it bloomed in early spring
—a sign of ground thaw—
                    meaning
the time had come to bury the winter
dead, that the circuit-riding preachers
would begin their rounds once more.

Today is May Day, Lei Day
where I'm from, but here where I am
Grandmother March extended her stay
well into April,
                foregrounding these
petals of the serviceberry's blossoms,
long and delicate flutterings that call
to mind an image I've seen

of handkerchiefs waving Susan B.
at the podium on. In another month
berries in clusters will ripen red
to blue to purple
                    into a deep blue black
as today, elsewhere, so many
people are lining the streets
on May Day. May Day.


Indigenous to North America—
Native peoples dried its berries
for pemmican. Serviceable, too,
for the handles of tools
                    and fishing
rods, its wood, which one tribe
sheared into panels they used
as a kind of body armor.


I'd seen but didn't know "shadbush"
(it blooms when the shad run)
now an ornamental. Come fall
how it burns a fiery red.
                    The word
"ornamental" brings to mind
a woman in the Mississippi Delta
asking a woman also from the Delta,

"Are you ornamental?" The brief silence
that followed the telling by the latter
woman—some stories are too deep
for tears.
           It's in the curve her lips make
after she turns her gaze down.
It's May Day, and I'm trying to gather
my scattered attention. Blessings

on the Amelanchier, one of the tribe
Maleae, the family Rosaceae, for, spring
and summer, its mystery of forbidden
fruit and transient beauty;
                    come fall
for cultivars like Autumn Brilliance
and Standing Ovation; for the serviceberry's
(the sugarplum's) fruit carried over

into winter, hard and dry and
humbled, bearing within it a hint
of almonds and the memory of summer.

# OUT OF BO(U)NDS

*. . . to humanise even the enemy*
—Mahmoud Darwish

When you put up a wall, you've effectively drawn
two sides. If you add four more, you can create
a space that will shape what does and doesn't belong
inside—moths, for example, or flies, gnats.

Adding to two sides four more will complicate
any argument. No doubt, you'll have made a wilderness
that discloses, like moths, flies, or gnats,
a shape to repulse the mind. Call it a tangled mess

because when argument sprawls into a wilderness,
someone will often call for Ockham's razor to simplify
into an easily apprehended shape that tangled mess—
think hair tamed by a blunt cut. No more beehives.

When calling on Ockham's razor to simplify,
why not also invoke that other blade, the guillotine.
No hair splitting—or, rather, one clean cut. The beehive's
contentious buzzing will stop. Like that, finé.

Sometimes people invoke knowledge, like a guillotine.
(A real discussion stopper.) How can one not feel snake bit
by the venom of gossip that ensues. Like that, finé,
a self-appointed umpire has called the third strike: Out.

Knowledge can sting. How does one not feel snake bit?
It's a story going all the way back to Eden with God
a designated umpire-in-chief calling the third strike: Out.
No Great Writ for this story of possessed, clay-hewn bodies.

In one version of the story of paradise, preachers cast God
as a father who, prizing above all else obedience,
claims absolute possession of his children's bodies,
thus setting the bar for their very un-Edenic existence.

In the name of a fatherland prizing obedience
a guard at the Juarez/El Paso border scrutinizes passports,
stripping the holder, honest or not, of her own existence.
In a game of us and them, it's sadly a full-court press.

Long ago, a customs officer eyed my driver's license,
said, "You don't look American." I know an Asian Asian
playing this game would mark me in an instant
by my slouch. What did I do? I smiled, said nothing.

I'm obviously not all-American. I'm not Hawaiian
either though the fact is, I grew up near Papakolea,
a slouch, an outsider who rarely smiled, said nothing
in a world that was bewilderingly multi-layered.

I was a neither, growing up near Papakolea.
See how early the via negativa circumscribed my life,
raised as I was in a world so deeply multi-layered,
nothing anyone tells me about it can quite describe it.

A playwright's via negativa begins with a polished script.
Later, the fourth wall, a curtain, opens, is a window.
Everything said or done on stage becomes inscription
of the interior's hall of mirrors and its shadows.

Imagination can turn a fourth wall into a window,
make of the mind a theater where everything belongs.
Shining its light in dimly lit places, it dispels shadows.
It is the well inside the self from which we must draw.

# PUNCHBOWL

*The light that puts out our eyes is darkness to us.*
　　　　　　　　　　　　　　—Thoreau


Here in this theatre under the stars,
　　　Ernie Pyle's marked grave is only one
among thousands of others simply marked UNKNOWN.
　　　But long before they were all killed
　　　along the Pacific Rim, another drama unfolded,

　　a bleak reminder of what seems
　　　　the unkillable law: Some thing must die
that others might live. Here was the place
　　of sacrifice, the bodies of law breakers,
drowned below in a pond, borne up to the crater

and placed on a stone slab—some left alone,
　　　some reduced to ash and bone that the family
　　gathered up and carried home. On the slopes
　　　　of this crater, I saw the after-effect of slaughter
　　on a small scale—some mongoose or stray

　　had found its way into my brother's pigeon coop
　　　and scattered the flock that never came back.
Memory blinks, and the smell of pigeon shit, blood is
　　　conjured up, the featherless skin of hatchlings turning
rubbery where they hung on perches or fell.

The road to the now-locked gate branches off to
        "homestead" land, so called so we can forget
    the place. They say the crater's extinct,
            the Pacific plate grinding steadily northward,
        but who can really know or say for sure what stirs


        under the surface? The inexorable law of bodies
            tells us no two can occupy the same space.
    Some must leave that others might live. *Go back*
        *where you came from.* But there's no there there
to return to. Tonight I have climbed from my father's house


up over the rim and descended into the crater to lie,
        sober, among the dead. This glimpse of the past—
    it's like looking at stars: Once you know what you're seeing,
            the hour of innocence is past. The light of dying stars
        puts out our eyes. Again and again in the dark,


    we stumble. We stumble and fall. And yet,
as if certain we know where we are, we get up.

# BROKEN

Pressed by the skillet's weight
the blue plate pitched from the drainer
and shattered. I picked up the pieces,

swept up fragments, saying,
"There, now, rest." In that moment,
marking its fall, I was godly.

And yet who wouldn't want instead
to have nourished by serving,
to have grown hot or cool, to frame

what it held? Steaming water streamed
over the plate, reddened my hands
as I rinsed then watched it, helpless,

fall . . . the way each year on the eve
of New Year's day, a sorry quarrel
between one or another pair of brothers

abruptly brought the gathering
to a close, the women interposing
their worn bodies, saying,

"Let's go home." Every year,
some grievance surfaced,
something dark, ancestral.

Like the shattered pieces
of the plate, the family struck
against a floor that wanted give.

Come morning, my father,
having slept it off,
would return to himself

and tend his portion of earth
under a sunlit sky grown
clear, blue, and inviting.

In me, too, something is broken.
Here is the ground my hands work,
damp with my father's sweat.

# E PLURIBUS UNUM

Beyond the three-thirties or
snaking the bleachers or
wind sprints, thighs parallel
to the ground, that first month
of practice, once or twice
in a group of five, we headed out
to the flagpole at Punchbowl.
This last I understood
as one more example
of peer pressure
wearing one down
and only occasionally
lifting one up. From the back
one picked up one's pace;
once up front, one held the line.

We ran a warm-up lap before
leaving the track, our coach,
hands at his mouth for a megaphone,
shouting, "Keep the line tight."
And, "No talking." When we began
to file uphill, some were dragged
forward by others who were
soon having to half-step.
It took some time,
but we did find a rhythm.

On last night's news,
my mother tells me years later,
a report of a teenager
picked up at a bus stop,
driven up Round Top then raped
and stabbed fourteen times.
She'd crawled out to the road,
where a passerby pulled over,
called the police, then
cradled her as she died.
"You w'en practice up dere, yeah?"

Back then, I preferred
running long distance
alone. In a Western I'd read
was a scene describing a narrow
trail shaped by and shaping
the inline stride of braves.
I wanted to move like that.
I worked on making my tracks
a single line. Even now,
in wide-toed boots my instep
sometimes grazes my instep.
How ironic, then, this lesson
in leading and following
that kept us safe,
was called Indian file.
I wish we'd done more of it.

# THE CORD

Hard to throw off old habits:
*ti* leaves tied to the front door,

the salt BaBa, come home
from a funeral, tossed over her shoulders,

the incense and food we offered the family
dead whom we burned and kept with us.

That was the world I lived in. Small wonder
each time I fly I watch the plane lift off

as if helping a thing get past inertia
is what we are born for. To bear

my son I bore down, and down
he fell until he emerged, head first,

the doctor turning him upright
and laying him on my belly.

For nine months, I'd known firsthand
evidence of the unseen. A thin coat

of blood made the cord, still uncut,
glisten. Thick and twined as rope

but translucent, it heaved
like something dying. You could say

I had suffered, labored under the curse
God laid on Eve's head.

But when the doctor severed
the cord, we had both suffered. Already

folding himself against the world,
he whimpered. And though I owed him

nothing, I put the child to breast.

# ON FIRST LOOKING INTO HONGO'S *VOLCANO*

When I was a child, we crisscrossed the seam
between two worlds, *kapu*ing the last popsicle
at a leisurely stroll.
        We *kapu*ed this,
that, not quite understanding
what the word meant. Sometimes

the word became synonymous
with "save": "Eh, I gotta go batch-room,
*kapu* one seat for me."
        Commoners all,
each of us could rise for a moment to *ali'i*.
Looking back, the strange part is

how long we honored it,
lived bone deep in the sphere
a single word evoked.
        Inevitably,
someone got greedy, collapsed
the axis between word and deed

by cheapening it. We found ourselves
racing, then mired in the tough-shit,
wop-your-jaws-
        I-got-'um-first
world of Do. *Do.* A scene
from the L.A. riots that stirred

feelings I couldn't articulate
played back in my mind for months:
A Black cleric,

        hallows a space,
his hand tracing a flat circle above
a Latino stunned on the curb,


his private parts spray-painted black.
Doing it, three men had said, "There
you're just like us."

           Now, they stand
paralyzed. I'd forgotten what held them.
Today, reading of lava tubes, I think of

that long-ago world, *kapu* it.

# CHANTICLEER

We change their names to forget we're eating
cow or pig flesh, but not so with chicken or fish,
as if some line had been drawn across the food chain.
How casually we say, "Crazy as a chicken
with its head cut off." My cousin had a rooster,
all white, its growth seemingly stunted, that pecked
all day at its own breast until the bleeding and scabbing
looked like a heart rising into its throat—the maudlin poet.
It never crowed. "Too strange," was the final judgment,
and my grandmother ate it, as she did my pet rooster.
Waste not, and so both birds were dispatched unnamed.
That rooster I raised as a teen was a crazy son-of-a-bitch.
At night I locked him in a cage my father made from the shell
of an old stove to keep him safe from neighborhood strays.
Each morning was a contest. He woke in a fury, flinging
himself against the mesh like my heart against its cage
during our morning ritual. I'd unbolt the lock
and tap on the cage then take off running
toward the front door, and he, having kicked
open the cage door, half flying, would be at my heels
like all of my unnamed demons loosed
by the time I reached the halfway mark of the stairs.
He would have attacked if he'd caught me
before my feet touched the front porch,
which was where he backed off. I know
because one afternoon he flew at a cousin's face
claws first and struck at her chest. I can imagine it,
his creamy neck feathers bristling above his iridescent
blue and green and red feathers. Two days later
my grandmother ate him. I don't know why
I never named him. Perhaps each of these unnamed

birds is a metaphor for what poetry might make of us.
But a story my mother recently told me offers yet another choice:
Long after I left, another rooster, owned by no one,
came to inhabit the neighborhood, drifting
from yard to yard, eluding cats and dogs,
and crowing at 4 o'clock morning or evening
or whenever. Everything about him was large,
wattles and comb, a strapping and virile youth
he might have been called were he human,
my pet rooster come back from the dead on steroids.
I know because I saw him perched on the lychee tree.
Over time Rooster became his name.
Crossing fence lines and boundaries, he was
the visible needle's eye, his exploits and whereabouts
the thread that held the neighbors together.
Till a man newly moved in to the neighborhood,
his routine having been disrupted one too many times
by this broken alarm, wrangled permission to trespass
—what was this after all, a chicken ranging free
on the edge of a city? He told Masako, the neighbor,
he meant to catch the bird who'd too long evaded
their lures and traps, and turn it over to Animal Control.
What argument was there, she thought, against zoning laws?
He entered her yard with a .22 and shot him. Stunned,
Masako held him, till my mother, who'd heard
the shot, returned with a shovel, and they buried him.
By then, eating Rooster would have been unthinkable.

# "TOTEM: AMERICA"

*—de Cordova Sculpture Park*

We're talking the rich pleasure
of simple foods, elegance
of pesto, of freshly baked bread,
your taste of Italy still lingering
as we approach a tower

of wire mesh squared
to hold together three by three
by twenty-four feet
of orange traffic cones,
soda cans, milk gallon-jugs, water bottles,

plastic fish crates, a tennis racquet,
detergent and bleach containers
with handles snipped, a football.
We walk slow circles around it.
I tell you the little I know:

the creator, a Russian immigrant
named Konstantin Simun,
gathering trash in his yard—
*valuable stuff*, he says—much
to the consternation of his neighbors.

*Vermin and filth*, they warn.
But your quick eye catches on a baseball,
seams ripped to form the brim
of a baseball cap, and under it,
for a face, the stars and stripes.

"See," you say. "A tongue, too.
Maybe it's his view of us."
When I look, yes,
what I see is a spoiled boy.
And when we step back

I can see the inverted cone like a vase
with its colorful spray of aluminum cans.
And from the big mouth cut into
one container spills bottles and cans.
As we take a few steps

farther back, on every side,
we see white and orange and blue and translucent
faces staring back. As we turn
away, what catches my eye, corralled in
near the pregnant Nefertiti,

is a pair of plastic containers
spray painted black, the bottom
one's mouth facing out,
a horn's bell—he's playing
a sax.

# THE MAN WITH THE RED GUITAR

lives a double life. By day
the scarf he wears maps the landscape:
a desert, an inlay of thick brown roads,
and, barely perceptible,
the red lines of his intent.

*

Backlit, a moving silhouette,
he enters the corridor. There
only the memory of the red guitar
slung over his shoulder keeps him upright.
In the light of an open door
he becomes himself.

*

It's the shock of artificial green
he hates, four windowless walls
and the low white ceiling.
He pulls a book from a wall
of books, and in it, concedes his heart.

*

Some nights, after work,
he lets the red guitar repose against him
like a close friend whose elbow
rests on the sofa's arm, waist curved
around him. He asks nothing more
than that it be there. After work

\*

some nights, he imagines the red guitar's
darkly silent mouth is his own
and won't even look at it.
The red guitar pools like a shadow
at his feet. Some nights

\*

he pulls the red guitar
from the trunk of his car, reclines
the passenger's seat, straps in
the red guitar, and opens the windows.
Light comes through the moon roof.
The fine hairs on his arms lift.

\*

He hums with the red guitar
when the wind brushes its strings.
Everything comes into focus:
the sky's orange and blue gradations,
the crisp line of mountains,
the eyes of animals winking
out of the dark, the line marking
the shoulder he'll follow all night.

# ON THE ANNIVERSARY OF OUR DEATH

I am wondering what to make
of your hands, their thick fingers,

thin, ridged nails unfailingly trimmed,
on the fleshy horizons, moons rising, eight?

—exactly how many, already I cannot remember—
the white-gold ring on your ring finger

as uncomfortably snug as your favorite
dress shirt's top button buttoned.

In my favorite photograph, your large
hands, whose fingers could grip a slip

of a pen—like a stir stick in mine—or type
long notes on the Palm's unfolded keyboard,

hang loose at your sides, cupping the dry air.
With Boyer and Sputnik off Highway 50,

its seemingly endless stretches of straight
road inviting speed, you'd pulled the Shadow

over, just past where the road eased
out of a curve, where Nevada's starkness

was a mirror catching the heart's
unquenchable thirsting for home.

I know the place—what need
for us to name it, then? And yet

at noon, in dark glasses and baseball cap,
you remain after thirty-six years still

a mystery. Your wedding ring, the key
to your Shadow, a five-yen piece

strung on a bead chain I wear
are dog tags, charms to ward off the cold,

cold things once warm in your hands.

# SONG OF THE TASTES

*And I saw my reflection in the snow covered hills*
*Till the landslide brought me down.*

—Stevie Nicks


I.   BITTERNESS


*Manini*, you might call these sorry sonnets
three-and-a-half years—on Father's Day—
late. I've been working to keep at bay
one more unexpected blow. Gunfunit!
I'm imagining the mango's leafy bonnet
as your gaze turned from the sky. It's hazy
today, sun occluded, everything gray—
like our darker selves, maybe "borned it."

Or maybe it was borne of the world's gradual
abrading of a child's pliable faith
worn finally too thin, like the soles
of the sneakers you, in haste, left on.
You, untethered above ladder and branch, fell,
the ground the same hard one you gave your life to.

## II.   SOURNESS

The same ground you gave your life to
was the very one I had to
leave. And only in retrospect
can I see that time as a kind
of training in reading perfection
beyond the unruly, unrefined
life we knew—though the yard you gave
your leisure to was a metaphor
for imagined beauty's fate. Save
for the avocado Grandma planted before
I was born, it was army worms, weeds,
mingled odors of fruits, flowers,
and excrement of dogs we needed
to ward off intruders at odd hours.

III.　SALTINESS

When my sailor came courting at odd hours,
he appeared your worst nightmare, I guess,
though later you'd deem him "one good *haole*."

In between, no one could predict I'd enlist
in the Air Force, not even me. Truth be told,
he had nothing to do with that. I think you must

have stood there, sucked in your breath and rolled
your eyes when Mom said your crazy daughter
had chosen her path to motherhood by soiling

your good name in dress blues. I wish I'd *been* wild.
But, no, he was my onliest. I couldn't get beneath
the straitjacket of family from which I'd exiled

myself. It was burned in, deep, like the tan lines, left
by the short-sleeved, V-neck T-shirts you wore, on or off

—no. No. In the wake of the tsunami of his death,
it made a space between waves where I caught my breath.

IV.   UMAMI (SAVORINESS)


In the space between waves of grief, I sometimes
sat outside the rented house and sipped a beer
after an afternoon of yard work. Clearly,
I was a prodigal almost-son coming home.
I understand. Nothing quite equals wind combing
fine hairs as skin cools, body at rest, mind clear
of the weight it must bear. To be here.
What you allowed yourself, I claimed as mine.

Call me bohemian. This is the paradox
of your legacy—your restlessness expressing
itself in perpetual motion, whether raking
or driving out and back to the Pearl or testing
a circuit board you built, in me is often noxious.
Still, we both lived by the book—as best we could.

V.  PIQUANCY


Of life, from a book: *Character is fate.*
   I prefer it over a friend's version:
      *The life you live is the life you will live.*
It's a reminder not to underestimate
   circumstance, invites small change even
      for one like me, bivouacked by accidents


of birth (mine) and death (yours). I'm here, you're not—
   Just like that. Let's consider calling them
      instead of tragedies a kind of pickle. Agreed?
Think the inexperienced tongue's first taste of
   kimchee.

VI.   SWEETNESS


It isn't kimchee, Father, I think of, now, when
I think of you, but the coconut cake you brought
home for my birthday; or your saying, *no scared 'um*—
six boxes of chocolate-covered macadamia nuts—

you'd heard your son-in-law call them divine;
or on the radio always when you set the dial,
slack-key—I'm only now moved by what KINE
played, deafened as I was by KPOI's rock 'n' roll;

and, last, the bittersweetness of BaBa's funeral:
Because I was practiced in public speaking,
I became the eulogist who read some poems. Fateful—
that's how it feels—having seen on your face a look

so rare and knowing my poems had put it there.
*Manini*, maybe, but enough, as I pray these are.

# LADY'S SLIPPER

It's a pretty photograph,
I thought, decorative as
a silk rose in its neat frame

until I encountered
a photographer lugging
camera and tripod,

a bagful of lenses in muddy,
ankle-wrenching terrain—
roots and rocks, dips and stumps.

It had taken days of aimless
wandering, he said,
of simply looking . . .

as now I remember your wonder
at those first photographs
beamed back from Spirit

and Opportunity. Far too driven
by deadlines, I stood
at your shoulder and stared

at the screen. What, I thought,
no moonsuits, no moon walking,
no one giant step as through

Spirit's lens we caught
a glimpse of Opportunity
looking rather insect like,

we agreed, you clicking
slowly through the images
they gave us, in each

an eerie glow like the mercury-
vapor haze we'd seen
at 2:00 am, Dealy Plaza, 1975.

*Mars,* you said. *That's Mars.*

# THE WAIT

*after Marc Chagall's* Waiting

Light touches the cow
the man touches, and

light is the man's touch
on the cow whose eye

says, *See the tether
I am,* says, *I know*

*what I know.* Its eye
and inward-turned horns

point to the yellow
rooster, doused in blue,

whose quizzical eye
gives nothing away.

Without the rooster's
tenuous hold would

the bride float away?
Over the village

below, a quarter moon
ascends. Eclipsed blue,

a bird keeps vigil
above a black cat

circling the well's rim.
A woman wearing

a yellow blouse and
blue skirt has returned.

What she's borne back
gladdens her pale horse

come to the barn door—
this much is certain.

Inside the village
hearth fires, long lit,

cling to blackened pots
worn spoons stir and sound.

Heat and scent and light—
everything rises.

The lost bride's bouquet
won't fade. Reduced to

gesture, is it her
heart or breast she means

to touch? *I'm cold*, she
seems to say. What if

she's saying, *Let go*?
Set off by his dark

hat and red shirt, gaze
lifted up, the man's

face is so pale. He
smiles, wills the light he

touches to touch her too.

# JUNIPER

Three days past the equinox,
here by a window, again,
reading *Eternity's Woods*
because a friend asked me to,
though, with my *somber*
*faith resembling*
*hope*, it isn't a river
and distant hills I see
but three pines, bare branches
of deciduous trees,
and one crow in a wash
of undivided blue.

For two days it had rained,
so it isn't hard to figure out
why only one bare tree,
a little sheltered by a pine,
is deeply tinged
with a leaf bud's coral.
Outside the window
a stop sign and farther out
across the parking lot
the stars and stripes measured
by the wind. Once I believed
in the permanence of mountains,
a wild horse against which
a man might test himself. Now
I know how fragile they are.
Now we break, we blast them
for a vein of coal.

Last week, flying into
the Springs, the sight
of snow-capped peaks
and there it was:
from deep within me
that audible indrawn breath
and the silence one hears
afterwards in the seemingly
inconsolable child—a chance
encounter drawing her back.
The next day, Fred and I
would walk the rimrock
of the outcropping
I stared and stared at
from the kitchen window.
It was that close.

Out past the oil rigs
and platforms, past
tires and plastic bottles,
the ATV tracks,
a makeshift campsite
draped in a sheet,
we walked. The first time
the trail dropped steeply,
he said, "Walk like a duck—
short, wide steps
to slow you down."
I'd heard it before.

Falling in behind him,
I saw evidence
of the stroke, how
he lifted his right foot,
toe close to the ground
for a moment before
the heel touched down—
as a dog or coyote might.

Here was his esplanade
of wind and cliff edge
carved by water, where,
he told me, rock doves nest,
where jays might fly
from tree to scrubby tree
as if to light his walk.
When, pointing, I asked,
he gave me a name:
Strawberry cactus.
He bent a little
to break off juniper needles,
rubbing them between his palms,
then lifting his cupped hands
up to my face
as if holding a bird
he'd plucked from the air.
"Out here," he said,
"in this high desert,
by reason of water,
of wind and soil,
no two give off
exactly the same scent."

There, the air so clear,
unaided he could hear
and speak beyond
the *crabbed masculinity*
of what he has been—
warrior and hunter, country
son of the ravaged city
of Flint, father of the man
I loved, who, now living
among the dead, yet
walks between us
when the trail levels,
sometimes holding our hands.
Even with all the stories I've heard,
what do I really know
of where they have been.

# THE BANANA TREE

Aimless as I am
I could never have found it
on my own, nor find

what is found there:
under a canopy of tall trees
a black-leaved sapling turned

willow, beside which my root
sinks so deep, I might believe
I'd emerged somewhere in China,

my guide a man made honorary mare
by a cow's gift of a heart valve.
Say that Old Horse is the very Earth.

Say that very green upturned
five-gallon plastic bucket
is a tortoise on which I sat

beside that wiry man holding
his staff—it's a snake, you know,
old as the one Moses owned.

With the one I borrowed,
it's leaning against a tree.
From his vest pocket,

two bananas. I eat one.
The peels lie on my thigh
like beached octopi in the quiet

of that uncertain place.
One at a time, he picks up
the peels by the stem end,

hangs each on a bare spot
of the banana tree—ah!—
laughing now, I am

beside myself, eyes tearing
for everything taken
and given, alive again

in the memory of it,
in the pale fresh peels
like blossoms,

like the bird's beak
of my hand not yet closed
in Single Whip,

in those soon-to-be
new leaves, draped as if
brought forth from within

and sprung from the branch,
each taking its place
among the others gone black.

# ANTENNAS

*after a photograph*
*by Dore Gardner*

Because I am neither here nor there,
I can stop if I want to. Like a horse,
I can sleep standing. This once
I'll ignore the power lines'
insistent hum. I know if I keep
those mountains on my right
I am always found. Up ahead
on Bell Hill I can visit the Cross
or stand below our three antennas.
Turning and turning, I'll be able to see
the whole of Sun City. But today
I am wearing my pilgrim's clothes.
On the road I can think that yucca up ahead
has bloomed for my sake. Can think
for the sake of my feet shod in cloth shoes
those pebbles and stones have cleared the road.
See how this tree behind me bent
to embrace me. Because I was weary.
Because I am neither here nor there.
Because no one's here.

# SONG

Goldfinches—they were—
not yellow leaves—four
drawn up
into the trees—a blur,
black-laced raw color
borne up.
I was thunked, word-stirred:
*Sunlight, sunlight, bird.*

Willow, widow, her-
self, my self once more
borne out
in the late light shorn
from summer forward,
drawn out:
not yellow leaves—four
goldfinches they were.

# Notes

p. 15: *"Irashaimasse"* is a greeting used by shopkeepers in Japan that means "Welcome!"

p. 22: "Ode to the Brown-headed Cowbird" was inspired by Yusef Komunyakaa's "Ode to the Maggot" in *Talking Dirty to the Gods* (FSG, 2001: p. 10).

p. 25: The opening stanza of "The Bog" refers to Constantin Brancusi's *Mademoiselle Pogany I*, 1913.

p. 27: "Confessional" was written in response to both an incident that occurred on a San Francisco MUNI Bus in October of 2009 and subsequent responses to the incident.

p. 30: "An Open Eye" is in memory of Don Belton.

p. 37: "Hit" was written after seeing a short video clip of Bill Iffrig near the finish line of the Boston Marathon on 15 April 2013.

p. 39: The first epigraph for "'Of Thee I Sing'" is from "Tragedy's Aftermath: Rage, Fear, Suspicion" by David Maraniss, published on 21 April 1995 in *The Washington Post* on page A20. The second epigraph is from James Merrill's "Elizabeth Bishop, 1911-1979," in *Elizabeth Bishop and Her Art*, edited by Lloyd Schwartz and Sybil P. Estes (U of Michigan P, 1983: p. 261).

p. 43: "Filigree" grew out of a prompt from Jae Newman.

p. 50: "Readings," written sometime after 9/11 and as we were both leaving Massachusetts, is for Laure-Anne Bosselaar.

p. 53: The title, "Blue Sky with Koi," was inspired by Eugene Gloria's title "Blue Sky with Thieves" in *Hoodlum Birds* (Penguin, 2006: p. 79). I owe the setting of this poem, the Missouri Botanical Garden, to Richard Newman.

p. 57: "May Day" is for Robin Lippincott. The anecdote about the word "ornamental" is from "The Untold Story of America's Southern Chinese," Part 2 of AJ+'s *Chinese Cuisine: An All-American Cuisine*, published on YouTube on 16 August 2017.

p. 60: The epigraph for "Out of Bo(u)nds" is from "Poet of the Arab World," a profile of Mahmoud Darwish by Maya Jaggi, published online in *The Guardian* on 8 June 2002.

p. 65: The epigraph for "Punchbowl" is part of the final paragraph in "Conclusion," the final chapter of *Walden*.

p. 69: *"E Pluribus Unum"* is for Joan Pong Linton.

p. 73: "On First Looking into Hongo's *Volcano*": The Los Angeles riots, as the 1992 event was referred to in the media then, was called "Sa-I-Gu" (four-two-nine) by Korean Americans—April 29—a date that coincided with the Jeju uprising in 1948. The poem's title refers to Garrett Hongo's *Volcano: A Memoir of Hawai'i* (Knopf, 1995).

p. 77: "Totem: America" is for Marilyn Miller.

p. 79: "The Man with the Red Guitar" is for Luke Whisnant.

p. 87: "Song of the Tastes": The epigraph is from "Landslide," a song written by Stevie Nicks. In the first section, I've borrowed the phrase "borned it" from Kunihiro Kaneda, who, according to Patrice Kaneda, used it often.

p. 98: "Juniper" is to Russ Kesler and for my late father-in-law Frederick P. Dean. The phrase "crabbed masculinity" is from "The Esplanade," and "somber faith resembling hope" is from "The River," poems by Paul Zweig published in *Eternity's Woods* (Wesleyan UP, 1985: pp. 8, 17).

p. 102: "The Banana Tree" was written for Almanzo "LaoMa" Lamoureux on his seventy-second birthday.

# Acknowledgments

These poems in *Totem: America* first appeared in the following print and online publications, sometimes in slightly different versions:

*Bamboo Ridge*: "Song of the Tastes"

*Café Solo*: "Readings"

*can we have our ball back*: "Single-lens Reflex" and "'Of Thee I Sing'"

*Connotation Press: An Online Artifact*: "Lady's Slipper" and "The Wait"

*The Florida Review*: "Blue Sky with Koi," "Ode to the Brown-headed Cowbird," and "On the Anniversary of Our Death"

*The Hampden-Sydney Review*: "Juniper" and "Song"

*The Louisville Review*: "The Bog," "Little Fly," "Medicine Ball," and "The Tongue Depressor"

*Luna*: "The Man with the Red Guitar" and "On First Looking into Hongo's *Volcano*"

*Many Mountains Moving*: "Burning. Love."

*Moon City Review*: "Out of Bo(u)nds"

*Mythium*: "*E Pluribus Unum*"

*One*: "The Banana Tree"

*Pluck!*: "Jam" and "Sweep"

*Prairie Schooner*: "The Cord"

*River Styx*: "Single-lens Reflex"

*Tar River Poetry*: "'Totem: America'"

"'Of Thee I Sing'" and "Punchbowl" appeared in *America! What's My Name?!: The "Other" Poets Unfurl the Flag*, Frank X. Walker, ed. (Wind Publications, 2007).

"Blue Sky with Koi," "Confessional," "Lady's Slipper," "Ode to the Brown-headed Cowbird," "Punchbowl," "Juniper," and "Song" appeared in *Fugitive Blues*, which won the 2013 Blue Moon Chapbook Contest (Moon City Press, 2014).

"Song" was featured on *Poetry Daily* on 1 November 2014.

"Broken" was translated into Korean and printed in English and Korean in *Reaching Out for Peace: Poetry for World Peace 2005* (Minumsa, 2005).

"Song" was featured on *Verse Daily* on 12 January 2011 and "Juniper" on 2 December 2014.

"Antennas" appeared in *Yellow as Tumeric, Fragrant as Cloves*, Anne Marie Fowler, ed. (Deep Bowl Press, 2008).

"Chanticleer" appeared in *Yobo: Korean American Writing in Hawai'i* (Bamboo Ridge Press, 2003).

With gratitude to Steve Huff for his faith in this book and to Phil Memmer for the care he has given in designing the cover and bringing the text into print; to Kathleen Driskell, Ross Gay, Eugene Gloria, and Tony Leuzzi for kindly reading and responding to it; and to Robin Lippincott for his help (understatement) with the cover art. My thanks to the editors who have supported my work through these long years. With love for my Spalding University and taiji communities, communities that have sustained me, and within them, abiding respect for Sena Jeter Naslund and Almanzo "LaoMa" Lamoureux. To Greg

Pape, Kathleen Driskell, Maureen Morehead, Molly Peacock, Jeanie Thompson, Roy Hoffman, Karen Mann, Crystal Wilkinson, and the late Rane Arroyo; to Selden Lamoureux, Violet Anderson, and Andrea Singer, Charles Pearce and Madeleine Gonin; and to Peter Makuck and Sarah Freligh—mahalo nui loa for reminding me where I am. To the Deans, of course. And to the Kangs, including my late father Kenneth and my late sister Allyson, and to my friend Annette Keliikoa—aloha for reminding me where I'm from. Though this book is dedicated to our son, Brad, for you, the watchword I keep: *wu wei*.

# About the Author

DEBRA KANG DEAN is the author of *News of Home* (1998) and *Precipitates* (2003), both from BOA Editions. She has also published *Back to Back* (1997) and *Fugitive Blues* (2014), both prize-winning chapbooks, and *Morning's Spell* (2013), a chapbook of renku written with Russ Kesler. Her poems have been featured on *Poetry Daily* and *Verse Daily*, and her essays are included in the expanded edition of *The Colors of Nature: Culture, Identity, and the Natural World* (2011) and in *Until Everything Is Continuous Again: American Poets on the Recent Work of W. S. Merwin* (2012). She teaches in Spalding University's low-residency MFA in Writing Program.

# *Colophon*

The text of *Totem: America* was set by Philip Memmer,
using Adobe Caslon Pro, Minion Pro, and Niagara Solid fonts.
The publisher is Steven Huff for Tiger Bark Press.

ॐ

Special thanks to the following individuals,
who contributed towards the publication of *Totem: America*:

Anonymous, in memory of Kurt Brown
Laure-Anne Bosselaar
Gregory Dean
Daniel DiStasio
Sarah Freligh
Sherman Kang
Almanzo Lamoureux
Peter and Phyllis Makuck
Timothy Millunzi
Jody and Joel Rich II
Andrea Singer
Barbara Thurston

## More Poetry from Tiger Bark Press

*After Morning Rain*, by Sam Hamill
*Meditation Archipelago*, by Tony Leuzzi
*Fancy's Orphan*, by George Drew
*Translucent When Fired*, by Deena Linett
*Ask Again Later*, by Nancy White
*Pricking*, by Jessica Cuello
*Dinner with Emerson*, by Wendy Mnookin
*As Long As We Are Not Alone*, by Israel Emiot,
translated by Leah Zazulyer
*Be Quiet*, by Kuno Raeber, translated by Stuart Friebert
*Psalter*, by Georgia Popoff
*Slow Mountain Train*, by Roger Greenwald
*The Burning Door*, by Tony Leuzzi
*I've Come This Far to Say Hello*, by Kurt Brown
*After That*, by Kathleen Aguero
*Crossing the Yellow River*, translated by Sam Hamill
*Night Garden*, by Judith Harris
*Time~Bound*, by Kurt Brown
*Sweet Weight*, by Kate Lynn Hibbard
*The Gate at Visby*, by Deena Linett
*River of Glass*, by Ann McGovern
*Inside Such Darkness*, by Virginia Slachman
*Transfiguration Begins at Home*, by Estha Weiner
*The Solvay Process*, by Martin Walls
*A Pilgrim into Silence*, by Karen Swenson